ICE CREAM

Written by
Jules Older

Illustrated by
Lyn Severance

SCHOLASTIC INC.

New York Toronto London Auckland Sydney
Mexico City New Delhi Hong Kong Buenos Aires

Jules and Lyn are giving 7.5 percent of their earnings on this book to Doctors Without Borders.

To my ice-cream-loving family: Effin (Vanilla Chocolate Swirl), Amber (Coffee, Coffee BuzzBuzzBuzz), and Willow (Chocolate Fudge Brownie). (My own fave flave is Coffee Almond Fudge.) —J. O.

In memory of Gramie, who first taught me how to make ice cream (Fresh Raspberry); and to Bill (Coffee Heath Bar Crunch), Jackson (Mint), and Henry (Chocolate), my ice cream-loving boys. —L.S.

A special thanks to Ed Marks, ice cream historian extraordinaire.
His favorite flavor is Toasted Almond Fudge.

The illustrations in this book were done with ink and Dr. Martin's Inks on Bristol board.
The display type was hand-lettered by Lyn and text type was set in Providence Sans.

Text copyright © 2002 by Jules Older.
Illustrations copyright © 2002 by Lyn Severance.
All rights reserved. Published by Scholastic Inc., 557 Broadway, New York, NY 10012, by arrangement with Charlesbridge Publishing.
Printed in the U.S.A.

ISBN 0-439-85606-X

5 6 7 8 9 10   08   14 13 12 11 10

Ice Cream

INCLUDING
GREAT MOMENTS IN ICE CREAM HISTORY

By Jules Older • Illustrated By Lyn Severance

📖 SCHOLASTIC

Part 1: Making It

Back In The Old Days, in cold places like Vermont and Montana, guys with big arms and sharp saws used to cut ice out of frozen lakes.

Yep,

they spent their winters cutting ice. Big blocks of ice. They'd save the blocks by covering them with sawdust and storing them in a cool, dry place. Like an underground icehouse.

When summer came, they'd scrape off the sawdust and break the ice into chips.

THEN They'd PuT Those ice chiPs ArounD The SiDes of an ice Cream Maker, Like Th

WHY DiD THey ADD SaLT To THe iCe ?

And then they'd add salt to the ice. I can already hear you asking, "Why did they add salt to the ice?"

Because

the salt makes the ice melt into slush. And to make ice cream, you want cold slush. Notice: It freezes stuff faster than ice would.

4

What about the cream?

Ah, the cream. Well, after they stuffed the ice and salt (remember, ice + salt = slush) around the ice cream maker, they poured cream into the ice cream maker. Cream and sugar and flavor.

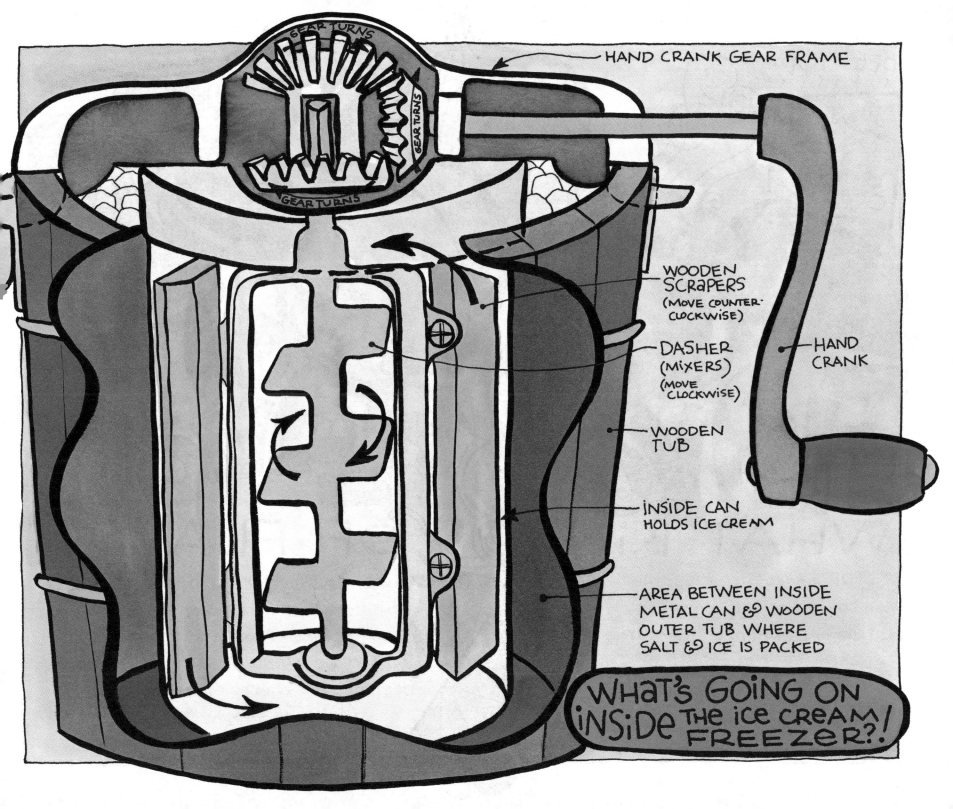

PEE YEW!

FLaVoR? FLaVoR?

WHAT KIND OF FLAVOR?

Oh, chocolate or vanilla or coffee or root beer or strawberry or peach or garlic or caramel or spaghetti or orange or lemon or smelly cheese. That kind of flavor.

Then they turned the crank on top of the ice cream maker and started mixing the cream and sugar and chocolate or vanilla or coffee or root beer or strawberry or peach or ~~garlic~~ or caramel or ~~spaghetti~~ or orange or lemon or ~~smelly cheese~~ flavor.

So that's how they made ice cream Back In The Old Days when your mother rode a horse to school, even in winter, and your dad was gonna grow up to be a cowboy.

& that's how they made it back in the days of black-and-white butter churns and TVs you had to crank by hand.

That's how they made it back when dinosaurs roamed the earth and people drove Volkswagen buses.

BUT—HOW DO We MaKe iCe CReam ToDaY?

HOW WE MAKE ICE CREAM TODAY

THERE'S HUNDREDS OF GALLONS IN HERE

MMMMM WHAT a LOT of GOOD EATiNG!

MIKE

ACTUALLY, we make ice cream pretty much the same way today. Sure, maybe an electric motor turns the ice cream maker instead of kids on a crank. And maybe we take the ice out of the freezer instead of the lake.

But other than little details like those, the rest of it is pretty much the same.

OH, EXCEPT

that you can skip the whole making-ice-cream business and stroll down to the corner and buy some ice cream that a great big company has already made.

If you can,

take a   company tour. You'll see thousands of pieces of chocolate getting stirred into oceans of vanilla. You'll smell cream and sugar and vanilla. You'll taste the free samples they hand out at the end of the tour!

THOSE ARE THE BASICS OF ICE CREAM MAKING. NOW GET READY FOR...

Ice Cream

long goes back a thousand the Roman sent big way. Almost two years ago, emperor Nero guys with strong backs to the Apennine mountains to haul snow to Rome so he could enjoy some honey ice and fruit ice and maybe a little wine ice in the hot Roman summers. Nero is famous for playing a fiddle while Rome burned.*

*But Nero couldn't have fiddled while Rome burned because . . . the fiddle hadn't been invented!

ROME

NO WAY!

64   100   200   300   400   500   600   700   800   900   1000

MARCO POLO
DIDN'T JUST BRING BACK SILKS & SPICES

Yes, the great thirteenth-century traveler also returned to Italy with recipes for "water ices." He told the amazed Italians that Asians had been making this stuff for thousands of years.

1100　1200　1300

NORTH AMERICA
ATLANTIC OCEAN
SOUTH AMERICA
SPICE ROUTE
AFRICA
FRANCE　EUROPE　ITALY

Ice Cream for the People!

No one's sure who first put the cream in ice cream. Marco Polo may have brought back a concoction that used yak's milk from China.

Between 1300 and 1600, somebody got the bright idea of adding cow's milk to the water ices. Some say it was the French; others swear it was Italians.

Until 1660*, ice cream was a treat reserved for the rich and famous: kings and queens and fiddly emperors like Nero. Then an Italian named Francesco Procopo dei Coltelli opened the Cafe Procope in Paris, where he started making big batches of ice cream for the rest of us.

*Or 1670. Or 1686. Ice cream experts can't make up their minds.

ASIA

POLO'S ROUTE

CHINA

PACIFIC OCEAN

IAN OCEAN

Café Procope

1500   1600   1660   1700

ICE CREAM COMES TO America

In 1744, William Black described a banquet prepared by the governor of Maryland, Thomas Bladen. About dessert, he wrote,

Among the rarities of which it was Compos'd, was some fine Ice Cream which, with the Strawberries and Milk, eat most Deliciously!

1700

1744

Vanilla Ice Cream

2 bottles of good cream
6 egg yolks
½ lb. sugar
1 stick of vanilla

THE COMING OF VANILLA

WHO WAS AMERICA'S 1ST BLACK ICE CREAM MANUFACTURER?

Thomas Jefferson may have been the first to bring vanilla ice cream to the United States, after he visited France. Here's his recipe:

JEFFERSON'S VANILLA ICE CREAM RECIPE!

THE WHITE HOUSE

Augustus Jackson was probably America's first black ice cream manufacturer. He made ice cream in the White House for Dolley Madison. After he retired as a White House chef, he made ice cream in Philadelphia in the 1820s.

1820's

Crankin'!

Augustus Jackson and everybody else made ice cream the hard way, constantly turning and scraping big pots filled with cream and sugar and chocolate or vanilla or coffee or root beer flavor. But in 1843, all that changed. An American named Nancy Johnson invented the hand-operated freezer. Now, instead of turning and scraping a pot, all you did was spin a crank until your arm fell off. Or felt like it did.

Nancy B. Johnson

1843

Ice Cream Goes Big Time

Only five years later, the United States had its first ice cream factory. It was opened by a milkman named Jacob Fussell* (rhymes with muscle) in Pennsylvania. He moved it to Baltimore, Maryland, two years later.

*Fussell was no ordinary milkman. He was a radical abolitionist who gave such fiery speeches against slavery that a mob of his Maryland neighbors offered to lynch him. When they burst in through the front door of his office, Fussell made a timely escape through the back.

PENNSYL 1ST VANIA

ICE CREAM FACTORY

1848

Who How & What

INVENTED Baked Alaska?

DID IT GET ITS NAME?

IS Baked Alaska Anyway?

Baked Alaska, first named omelette surprise, was invented by an American scientist named Benjamin Thompson in the late 1700s. Thomas Jefferson loved eating it. It got its name in 1867, in honor of the American purchase of Alaska.

Who named it Baked Alaska? Charles Ranhofer, the chef at Delmonico's restaurant in New York City.

What Is Baked Alaska? Well, ask your friends this question: "What's made of ice cream, cake, and meringue, all baked together?"

Then tell 'em the startling answer! And ask them why, if it's baked, it doesn't melt. (The answer: It's baked for only a few seconds.)

MERINGUE

2ND ICE CREAM FLAVOR

ICE CREAM

CAKE

1867

BiRTH OF THE Ice Cream Soda
THE TRUE STORY

It's 1874. Robert Green is making a crummy six dollars a day selling a mixture of syrup, cream, and carbonated water in Philadelphia. One day he runs out of cream. What does he do? He tosses in *ice cream* instead. Next thing you know, Robert Green is making six *hundred* dollars a day.

2 years later, the ice cream soda was introduced to the rest of the world at the 1876 Centennial Exposition, also in Philadelphia. There's a cool story about this fair on page 25. Don't miss it!

1874   1876

How the Ice Cream

Q:

Who invented the ice cream sundae?

A:

One story says it was Ed Berners in Two Rivers, Wisconsin, in 1881.* He made it out of ice cream topped with chocolate syrup.

WISCONSIN

1881

Sundae Got Its Name

Q: Why is it called a sundae?

A: Because, at first, Ed Berners made them only on Sundays.

Q: Then why is it called sundae instead of sunday? Couldn't he spell, or what?

A: Or what. Ed Berners could spell, all right. But the story goes that the pious people of Two Rivers found the word Sunday offensive when applied to something as sinfully rich as ice cream.

S UNDAY	M ONDAY	T UESDAY	W EDNESDAY	TH URSDAY	F RIDAY	S ATURDAY
			1	2	3	4
5	6	7	8	9	10	11
12	13	14	15	16	17	18
19	20	21	22	23	24	25

*Everybody wants to be the daddy of a winner. Other cities that claim, "The ice cream sundae was invented here!" are Buffalo and Ithaca, New York, and Evanston, Illinois.

SO NOW the ice cream soda & the ice cream sundae have been invented. WHAT COULD POSSIBLY BE NEXT?

THE Invention of the Ice Cream Cone

In 1896, Italian-American Italo Marchiony sold ice cream from a pushcart in New York. One day, after running out of bowls, he molded a warm waffle into a cup that you could eat. New Yorkers loved it.

WAFFLE IRON

1896

The first waffle cone was made by Ernest A. Hamwi at the 1904 World's Fair in St. Louis.* Mr. Hamwi, who had come to the United States from Syria, was selling zalabia, a skinny Persian waffle. Next door, a man was selling ice cream in dishes until, one busy afternoon, he ran out of dishes. So Mr. Hamwi wrapped a zalabia around a scoop of ice cream, and

SHAZAM!

the waffle cone was born.

*Other people claim they invented the waffle cone at the 1904 World's Fair. Ya pays yer money, ya takes yer choice.

ICK!   YUM!

1904

TIME WARP, TIME WARP, TIME WARP!

1876 Philadelphia Centennial Exposition

At the 1876 Philadelphia Centennial Exposition, the world's biggest soda fountain went on display. It stood 33 feet tall and weighed 30 tons. (A big African elephant weighs about 8 tons.)

WORLD'S BIGGEST SODA FOUNTAIN

SPLITTING THE BANANA

After two kinds of cones plus sodas and sundaes, the next great step in ice cream history was . . . The Banana Split! Here's the inside scoop:

The year? 1904. The place? Latrobe, Pennsylvania. The inventor? A young assistant in the Tassell Pharmacy named David Strickler. The recipe? Split a banana in half.

Place the halves, flat side down, along the sides of the dish. Remove peel. Plop three scoops of ice cream on top of the bananas. Top each scoop with a different topping. Spread the whole thing with whipped cream. Toss in a few more pieces of fruit. So let's have a big hand for David. . . . He split the banana and invented the banana split!

1904

YEAH DAVE!

What were the Greatest Years in Ice Cream History

The years 1920–1923, during which the Popsicle, the Eskimo Pie (ice cream in a chocolate shell), and the Good Humor bar (ice cream on a stick) were all invented. And the commissioner of Ellis Island invited all the immigrants to the United States who stopped off there to have ice cream for dessert at their first American meal.

1920–1923

POPSICLE

1920

LIBERTY

ESKIMO PIE

1923

WHOLE LOTTA SHAKIN' ICE CREAM FACTORIES

In 1937 Earl Prince invented the Prince Castle Multi-Mixer, which could make six milk shakes at the same time. In the ice cream world, things were shakin' and movin'.

But the biggest move was from little, itsy-bitsy ice cream makers in people's kitchens and in corner ice cream parlors to big, jinormous ice cream makers in factories. The world's biggest ice cream factory (I'm sure you want to know this) is in Bakersfield, California.

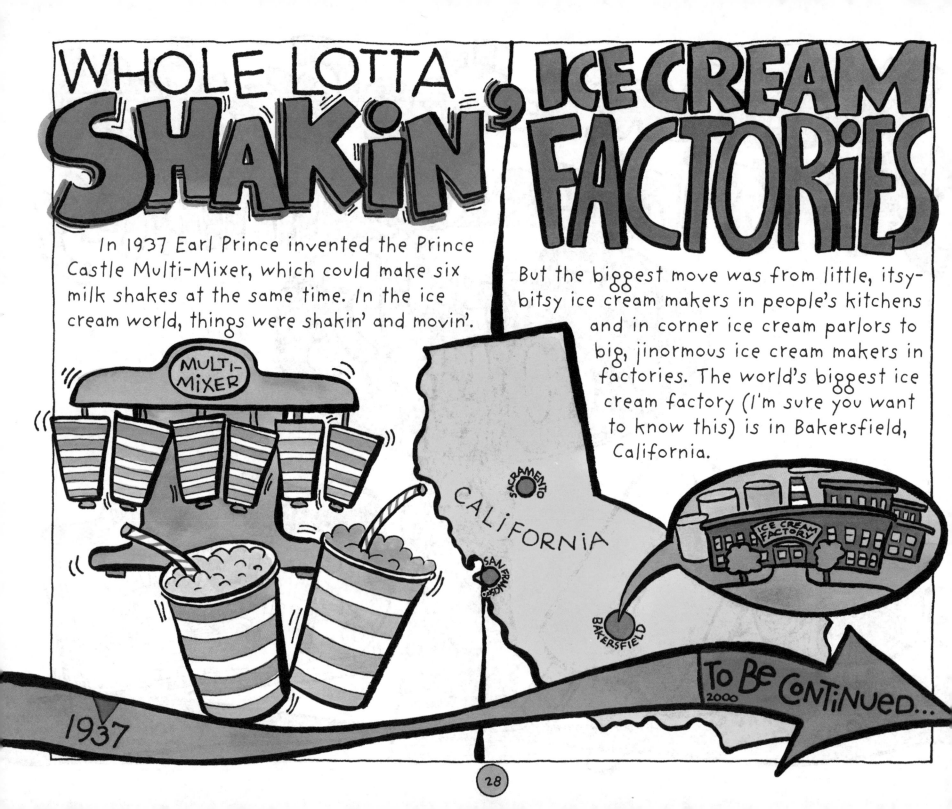

MULTI-MIXER

CALIFORNIA

SACRAMENTO

SAN FRANCISCO

BAKERSFIELD

ICE CREAM FACTORY

1937

TO BE CONTINUED...
2000

Part 3: What do YOU know About ice Cream?

So now you know about the ice and the cream in ice cream. You know how ice cream is made. You know the really true history of ice cream from Rome to California. Now we'll see what you **really** know about ice cream . . .

Name the top five ice-cream-eating countries in the world.

5. Sweden (edging out Canada*)
4. Australia (ending the Belgium and Luxembourg tie)
3. Finland (upsetting Denmark)
2. New Zealand (knocking out Finland)
1. The United States of America (now and forever!)**

*Canadians: You've dropped from fifth to seventh place. If you want to be in the top five, you've got to apply yourselves. Eat more ice cream!

**That's about fifteen quarts per American per year. Men eat more than women; adults eat more than kids.

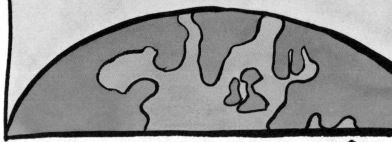

Name the top ice-cream-eating state.

In Utah, people eat more ice cream than in any other American state.

SALT LAKE CITY

UTAH

What's the most popular flavor?

Without a doubt, the number one, all-time winner and champeen flavor is (the envelope, please . . .) plain, old vanilla.

VANILLA BEAN

①

What's second?

Yeah, it's chocolate.* Then Neapolitan, which shouldn't be a surprise since it's made of vanilla and chocolate (and strawberry, too). Fruit flavors (like strawberry), nut flavors (like butter pecan), and candy mixes (like mint chip) come next. *Chocolate comes from the cacao tree, theobroma cacao (theobroma means "food of the gods"). It grows in hot, damp places like parts of Africa and the Amazon basin.

② ③ ④

What are the world's greatest flavor flops?

Here they are. These are actual flavors tested by leading ice cream companies. This is not stuff I've made up.

GOODY GOODY GUM DROP

PRUNE → YUCK!

LICORICE BLECH!

KUMQUAT

(This one tasted OK, but the gum drops froze and mangled your teeth.)

eee-ooo

LOX & BAGEL - NO WAY!

GROSS

KETC

CHILI ick!

Name, in order, the three most popular ice cream toppings.

Uno. Hot fudge.
Dos. Chocolate fudge.
Tres. Caramel.

What is the most unusual flavor of ice cream you can buy today?

The Most Unusual Flavor of Ice Cream You Can Buy Today is Lobster.

It contains:
a. Vanilla ice cream
b. Big chunks of real, recently alive lobster
  To taste this, uh, special treat, you need to go to Bar Harbor, Maine.

And that's it. Now you know the truth about ice cream. Including great moments in ice cream history. Plus, a tough quiz to find out what you know about ice cream.

So now you know everything about ice cream except one thing. Except one eensy-teensy-weensy, little thing:

How Does Ice Cream Taste?
There's only
              one way
                        to find out . . .

Books & Websites

BOOK LIST

Irena Chalmers, **Donvier Ice Cream**, Irena Chalmers Cookbook, 1986.

Ann Cooper Funderburg, **Chocolate, Strawberry, and Vanilla: A History of American Ice Cream**, Bowling Green State University, 1995.

Robert T. Marshall and W. S. Arbuckle, **Ice Cream**, fifth edition, Chapman & Hall, 1996.

Jill Norman, **Ice Cream & Sorbets: Frozen Delicacies to Please the Eye and Palate**, DIANE Publishing Company, 1998.

Jules Older, **Ben & Jerry—The Real Scoop!**, Chapters, 1993.

Jacki Passmore, **The Book of Ice Creams and Sorbets**, HP Books, 1986.

WEB SITES

www.ice-cream.org/school/index.htm
Ice Cream (Alliance) an Education
This site is packed full of ice cream jokes, puzzles, and facts. Learn more about your favorite dessert and have fun doing it!

www.cowtunes.com/history.html
Cow Tunes for Kids®
Check out the "unofficial" history of ice cream at the Cow Tunes site. As an extra treat you can download Cow Tunes—songs written about cows and ice cream.

www.kidsdomain.com/craft/icecream2.html
Kids Domain
There's more than one way to get ice cream—like making it yourself. This site tells you how to make ice cream in a coffee can and in a plastic bag.

THE END